IMAGES OF ENGLAND

KENDAL

PANNUS MIHI PANIS

IMAGES OF ENGLAND

KENDAL

ARTHUR NICHOLLS AND TREVOR HUGHES

The History Press

Frontispiece: Displayed in full colour on the parapet of Victoria Bridge in Sandes Avenue, the town's coat of arms comprises a quartered shield bearing representations of bale hooks and teasels, tools of the wool trade. The shield is mounted on a simulation of a hide. Together, they display the two main products on which the economy and wealth of Kendal were once based. This is exemplified by the motto, *Pannus Mihi Panis*, roughly translated as 'Wool is my bread'. The coat of arms originated in a badge of his own design placed on his map of Kendal in 1610 by John Speed. It was gradually adopted by the town as a coat of arms and remained in unauthorised use until 1993 when it was at last registered with the College of Heralds.

First published 2006
Reprinted 2011

The History Press
The Mill, Brimscombe Port,
Stroud, Gloucestershire, GL5 2QG
www.thehistorypress.co.uk

British Library Cataloguing in Publication Data.
A catalogue record for this book is available from the British Library.

ISBN 978 0 7524 4062 0

Typesetting and origination by The History Press
Printed in Great Britain

Contents

Acknowledgements

We would like to thank the following:

Kendal Library Local Studies Collection, Cumbria Record Office – Kendal, Kendal Town Council, *Westmorland Gazette*, Anne Thompson – Geoffrey Thompson Archive, Roger Atkinson, Marjorie Baker, Margaret Clarke, Delia Daws, Brian Dawson, Walter Dennison, Jim Graham, Stan O'Connor, Anne Pattison, Alan Thompson, David Willacy, Ian Woof.

Introduction

'The Gateway to the Lake District' was a term devised for Kendal as an exercise in advertising, but the slogan fell short of the mark as Kendal is far more than a gateway to somewhere else. It is a place of importance in its own right. A better sobriquet is 'The Auld Grey Town', its ancient buildings being coloured by the native limestone. Grey they may be, but Kendal is a vibrant market town, the most important in the old county of Westmorland – now South Lakeland.

When the first settlers came they found a place by a river crossing, a pleasant area in which to live and thrive, warmed by the Gulf Stream from the south and surrounded by hills around. A settlement grew up beside the swiftly flowing river Kent where a church was built to become the centre of the community which is named to this day Kirkland – the Church Land. The Romans established a fort – named Medibogdu – in the bow of the river, now known as Watercrook, and they eventually vanished with little to show for their time there. Anglian invaders too came and went leaving little or no trace. By the beginning of the Middle Ages a market town had also grown up north of Kirkland, the stream of Blind Beck marking the boundary between them. Kirkland and Market Kendal remained separate entities right up until 1908 and even today Kirkland retains its independent spirit.

The main road through Kendal runs from the higher lands in the north to lower lands in the south. The northern part is Stricklandgate and the other Highgate (previously Soutergate or the South Road). Where they join, in the centre of the town, a branch to the east runs through Finkle Street and Stramongate (the road to Scotland), and one from opposite the Town Hall stretches towards the west coast port of Whitehaven. The suffix 'gate' indicates a Norse or Viking derivation of the word 'road'. The western road was much used by packhorses and wagons carrying wool exports and tobacco imports.

Kendal received its first charter in AD 1189 from King Richard I authorising the holding of regular markets. These have been held in the Market Place every week to this day. A second charter was granted by Queen Elizabeth I creating the town a royal borough with a mayor and corporation. A Moot Hall was built to act as a Town Hall and court. Two further charters were granted by Charles I and Charles II which did little but confirm previous rights.

Fellside, the rising ground to the west side of the town, was a maze of narrow ginnels and cramped habitations known as 'The Ghetto of Kendal's Poor' where the houses and cottages were crammed together and where the poor lived and worked in a close-knit community. In the post-war euphoria of the 1960s most of Fellside and many of the yards were swept away and Kendal lost some of its ancient charm, though perhaps to the benefit of those who had lived there.

The River Kent has always exercised a dominant influence over the town. Rising in the Kentmere Valley and fed by its tributaries, the rivers Sprint, Mint and Gowan, it bisects the town, the earliest settlements being on its western bank. Falling some 2,000ft in only twenty miles, when in spate after heavy rain or melting snow, it moves extremely fast and, before the extensive work on it in the 1970s, often overflowed its banks, regularly flooding the lower-lying parts of the town. Five road bridges cross it, three of extreme age, still taking the modern heavy traffic. In its time the river served and powered numerous mills and factories along its banks. It was the receptacle of much noxious waste from industries such as tanning, together with house sewage in general, taking it out eventually into the Irish Sea in Morecambe Bay. Thankfully, those days are far gone and the river now flows sweetly.

The canal to Lancaster and Preston was opened in 1819 on the anniversary of the Battle of Waterloo. It served the town well for some twenty-eight years when the railway came, effectively supplanting it. The canal survived until the 1960s when it was filled in with industrial and domestic waste. Active plans are now in place to re-open it but this time mainly for recreational use. The railway from Oxenholme Junction to Windermere passed through Kendal. Prominent members of the town and Kendal Corporation endeavoured to persuade the planners of the Lancaster & Carlisle Railway to take its line through the town but to no avail and it remains merely a branch line to the lake town. In its heyday it served Kendal well, providing a means of carrying produce in bulk into and out of the town, passengers to the cities of Lancaster and Carlisle, excursionists into and out of the Lake District and local people to the watery delights of Bowness and Morecambe. As elsewhere in the country, the motor car and lorry have taken over those roles but the railway, reduced to a single line, continues to bring tourists into Kendal.

Until recent years Kendal was a hive of industry. Together with the major mills and manufactories there was a plethora of small factories and workshops producing a vast amount of varied goods. Sadly, the woollen industry and shoemaking have declined to oblivion and the town's economy is now more dependent on the service industry and tourism. However, it is still a bustling, lively market town which has never lost its rural roots. Poised on the edge of the Lake District National Park, Kendal remains an admirable stopping-off point as part of a holiday to the northern fells. At the same time, it is a town with a fascinating history and so much to see and explore.

one

Kirkland –
The Beginning

As with so many towns, the early history of Kendal is shrouded in mystery. A few occasional finds such as animal bones, a stone axe and querns for grinding corn have been unearthed. Traces of a Bronze Age burial site have been discovered on the southern edge of the town. All these give faint clues to life before written history.

Religion, both Pagan and Christian, played a major part in the growth of Kendal and this is where the story begins to be unrolled. It seems that the Anchorite Well may have been the very origin of the town. Christianity came to Kendal either through the Romans or by Celtic missionaries during the sixth or seventh centuries. During the Victorian restoration of the parish church some pieces of stone were discovered, thought to be part of an earlier Saxon church. The conflict between Roman Catholics and Protestants which ravaged the country had its effect in Kendal, as exemplified in the parish church, though not perhaps to the same extent as elsewhere. The spread of denominations resulted in many churches being built in the town and in the eighteenth century the Quakers, or Society of Friends, became dominant in the commercial and social life of the town. Quaker bankers were known for their honesty and dependability during a time of national financial crisis in the eighteenth century.

An ancient hill fort, Castlesteads, was established on the summit of a hill just outside the town which might possibly have been set up by a local group of the Iron Age *Brigantes* and later used by the Romans as a signal station. The influence of the Romans spread beyond their fort. It is certain that a market was formed where the hub of Roman roads brought trade into Kendal. The local community served the fort and to some extent integrated with its over-rulers. This aptitude has enabled Kendalians to adapt quietly to change. The Romans disappeared in the fourth century and the Dark Ages began, Kendal's history now being silent until it revived with the Normans.

The Anchorite Well above Kirkland is Kendal's oldest historic, religious site. Filled by a stream from Kendal Fell, it has never run dry, even in the hottest summer. Its supposed magical properties prompted worship of the earth mother. An anchorite or hermit lived there and a church was later built dedicated to St Mary, 'The Mother of God', which became a chantry, demolished when the parish church was built.

The parish church, dedicated to the Holy Trinity, was the centre of Kirkland. From early times, in the open village green near the church, a maypole was set up each May. It can be discerned in the centre of the picture. It was prohibited by the Puritans but returned with the Restoration and survived until 1792 when it caused an obstruction to the increasing traffic and was removed.

This part of Kirkland close to the parish church was once a village green where a maypole was erected as part of the ancient ceremony of maying. This was repressed by the Puritans and the maypole taken down but the festival lingered on for many years in the streets. The base of the maypole was unearthed in 1825 when laying gas mains but has since disappeared.

The parish church of Holy Trinity was built in the thirteenth century, possibly on the site of an earlier Saxon building. It was given to the Benedictine monks of St Mary's Abbey in York by the first Baron of Kendal, Ivo de Tailebois. Succeeding barons endowed the church with land so that it gained in importance and influence, dominating Kirkland physically and in government. The engraving shows Abbot Hall beside the church.

The parish church has endured many vicissitudes during its long life. In the thirteenth century it was desecrated in one of the periodic Scots border raids. After the dissolution of the monasteries the living, part of the tithes, the vicarage and some of the glebe land were given by Queen Mary to Trinity College in Cambridge. The church was extensively restored by the Victorians.

Right: The profits from wool trading enabled the church to be widened between the fourteenth and sixteenth centuries, making it the second widest parish church in the country. The Parr chapel contains the family tomb and a piece of an Anglian preaching cross. A memorial to George Romney, the artist, is near the font. On one wall are a helmet and sword, reminders of an exciting exploit during the Civil War.

Below: The Ring o'Bells is one of the few public houses on consecrated land. It was built by the sexton, John Fisher, in 1741 as a retreat for the churchwardens and bell-ringers. It has a second door conveniently facing the church porch providing easy access for the ringers. Until 1822 there was a set of stocks placed between the public house and the church gates to accommodate wrongdoers.

Above: Designed by George Webster, St George's church was opened in 1841 as a replacement for the old St George's chapel-of-ease. It was built on a raised platform some 6ft above the river to guard against the frequent flooding. It faced near-disaster in the floods of 1864 and 1898 when it stood as an island in a lake of flood water, but successfully survived the ordeal on both occasions.

Left: The church was built with spires on the towers flanking the entrance but the nature of the subsoil caused cracks in the stonework, making them unsafe, so they were removed in 1927. The church bell was removed in 1978 and the towers were reduced in height to avoid further damage. A modern porch has recently been added.

Above: With the growth of the town in the nineteenth century, the original parish was divided and a new church, designed by George Webster, was opened in 1837 to serve the north of the town. St Thomas's church was built with the altar facing west instead of east as the western end of the site, Fell Field by Dyers Beck, was too boggy to support the weight of the tower.

Right: The Presbyterians moved in 1897 from their outdated chapel in Woolpack Yard to the new St John's church in Sandes Avenue, designed by Stephen Shaw. Its lantern lectures were popular, one being 'Around Great Britain in a Yacht' which included views of Windermere! In 1980 it was closed, the congregation merging with the United Reformed Church in Highgate. It was demolished in 1982 and the site is now housing.

Above: The castle was less of a garrison than a fortified manor house, showing the inhabitants of the town who was in command and control. There is no evidence that it was ever attacked. The hall block provided the living and administrative accommodation for the baron and his servants. It contained a great chamber with a fine window, bedrooms and living quarters with garderobes, or lavatories, in the outer wall emptying into the ditch.

Left: The most famous family who owned and lived in the castle was the Parrs, in the fifteenth century. The most well-known member of the family is Katherine Parr, the sixth, last and surviving wife of King Henry VIII. Although she was related to the Stricklands of nearby Sizergh Castle, there is no evidence that she ever visited Kendal Castle and neither was she born there as local tradition still maintains.

Kendal Castle was built on its hill around 1200, possibly by the Baron of Kendal, Gilbert fitz Reinfred. Built of Silurian slate with some limestone and granite, on a limestone outcrop, it consists of a hall block within a curtain wall and towers, surrounded by a ditch across which entrance was effected by a bridge. The drawing by Todhunter is a fanciful attempt to show its original appearance.

The castle had become neglected by 1571 and was falling down with age. It was passed to the Crown and was systematically dismantled, the materials being sold off or purloined by thrifty local inhabitants. It became a romanticised ruin dominating the town skyline. It was bought by the Corporation, together with the hill, and opened as a public amenity to celebrate Queen Victoria's Diamond Jubilee in 1897.

Abbot Hall was a house used by the Abbot of St Mary's on his visits to the Abbey lands in Kendal. It was replaced in 1759 by the present Abbot Hall designed by John Carr of York for Colonel George Wilson of Dallam Tower. It was bought by the Corporation to celebrate Queen Victoria's Diamond Jubilee, became derelict and was later restored, becoming one of the country's leading art galleries.

To control the conquered population, William I established castles in salient positions. One such was Castle Howe on the western ridge above the town close to the ancient border with Strathclyde. A wooden defensive tower was raised on an earthen motte below which was a bailey for servicing the castle. When and why the castle was razed is unknown. The monument on the motte celebrates 'The Glorious Revolution' of 1688.

Following centuries of persecution, Roman Catholics opened their first church in the town on New Road, facing the river. Built by Webster in 1837 it has on its gable a statue by Thomas Duckett of St George slaying a dragon. With its name of Holy Trinity and St George, was this its comment on the old enmity between the Anglican church represented by Holy Trinity and St George churches?

Surrounded now by modern housing, the date when Pembroke House (Collinfield farmhouse) was built is unknown, but it was clearly an Elizabethan manor house. It was used by Countess Anne Pembroke as a rest house when she journeyed from Skipton to Appleby. She gave her private secretary, George Sedgwick, £200 towards buying the house around 1668. It has oak panelling and a secret hiding place, perhaps a priest hole.

Levens Bridge is at the junction of the present A6 road and that from Furness and West Cumberland where an old toll house once stood. The narrow bridge was of two spans. It was widened on the western side at the turn of the nineteenth century and, because of continually increasing traffic along what was the main road to Scotland, the eastern side received a still broader widening in 1931.

Levens Hall was built on the bank of the river Kent in the fourteenth century as a border pele tower to which a great hall was added. Some remains of the original house can still be found. It was sold to Alan Bellingham in 1489 and remained in his family until sold in 1688. He transformed the building into an Elizabethan mansion which is now owned by the Bagot family.

Over succeeding years the hall was altered and extended. In the seventeenth century the chapel was converted into a library and an enclosure under the staircase was railed off for daily family prayers. An alarming fire in the kitchens in 1788 damaged the ladies' chamber. Fortunately, they were not in their beds and no-one was hurt. Much of the kitchen equipment was ruined but the books and papers were saved.

Levens Hall is famous for its gardens which were laid out for Colonel Grahme by Monsieur Beaumont. He established the Topiary Garden in which the yew trees are clipped into fascinating shapes. Beech trees, some over 15ft tall were added later. The original shapes of the beds and borders have been kept virtually unchanged over the centuries. There have been only eight head gardeners in all that time.

The castellated Sizergh Castle originated as a pele tower in the fourteenth century to which a great hall was added. It has been inhabited by the Strickland family for some twenty generations. Tradition says that Katherine Parr slept in the 'Queen's Room' in the tower although the inscription over the fireplace, 1569 *Vivat Regina*, actually refers to Queen Elizabeth I.

Built as a pele tower in 1275, a stump of which survives, a house was added in the fourteenth century to form Burneside Hall where the Bellingham family lived for over 200 years. It has become somewhat derelict. The principal bedroom has a fine carved oak screen and is said to have been haunted. During Scots border raids cattle were driven for safety into a fortified walled enclosure.

two

The Auld
Grey Town

Kendal is a linear town. The river Kent runs through the centre, dividing it into two. The old main road was on the western side and a later one on the eastern, parallel to the river. Being a market town, the main roads were lined with both houses and shops. Leading from the roads on both sides were the many yards for which Kendal is famous. These yards were the homes and workshops of the working population. Their origin was in the burgage plots, land allocated in earlier days to the burgesses of the town who often built a house for themselves fronting the road, the yard extending to the river side or the fell side, being named after the owner. These yards were hives of activity in the nineteenth and part of the twentieth centuries. Sadly, the 1960s saw a wholesale demolition of many of them in part or the whole which, although essential on hygienic grounds, has been a distinct loss to the town. Those that are left remain to interest and intrigue visitors still.

At one time all traffic to Scotland passed through the town and until 1887 its only exit was through the narrow Finkle Street. The opening of Sandes Avenue in that year brought some relief but it was not until 1970, when the M6 motorway was opened, that the traffic problem was eased, although never solved completely. The streets each have their features of interest and the following pages will take you on a stroll through some of them.

The view from the air shows clearly the street pattern of the town with the castle looking down on it from its hill.

The old Cock and Dolphin Inn held for 200 years the honour of being the southernmost Kendal inn and has a place in the spurious legend of 'Dickie Doodle'. It was rebuilt about 1898 by which time Henry Wiper had been landlord for forty-four years. The Cock derives from the arms of the French royal family and the Dolphin from the title of the Dauphin.

Nether Bridge existed by at least the fourteenth century. It was at the lower end of the town and was a narrow toll bridge. The alcoves on the sides of the parapet were safe places to stand when packhorses went by. There was a ford beside the bridge for wagons. The bridge was widened in 1772 and again in 1908, signs of which can be seen under the arches.

Glebe Cottage was the lodge at the entrance of the tree-lined drive to Glebe House, the old vicarage. It was known to have been there in 1563 with the river ford beside it and was abandoned in 1860 when a new vicarage was opened elsewhere. It was demolished in 1910 when all the property from the bridge to the Ring o' Bells was pulled down.

A chantry school was founded in 1575 in the parish church. It was refounded as a grammar school in 1588 by the Phillipsons of Crook in this building beside the church. When the new grammar school was opened in 1889 the building was vacated and is now part of the Museum of Lakeland Life and Industry. Ephraim Chambers, who wrote the world's first encyclopaedia, was a boy at the school.

Above: Hogg's Yard is typical of Kendal's yards and was named after the principal resident, Alan Hogg, who lived at the head of it and ran a bakery there. The yard was densely occupied by poorer labouring families. The steps to the first door guarded against flooding from the river and the ground floor was used as a workshop.

Left: Chapel Lane was named after the ancient St Mary's chantry by the Anchorite Well and led from there to Kirkland. The lane was once lined with cottages and at least four public houses. It has also been called Capper Lane, said to refer to Thomas Capper who owned or built property there, but this might be mere coincidence. The lane has now been developed out of all recognition.

Cross Lane is one of the little streets behind Kirkland. The steps on the end of the building lead to the living accommodation above a workshop or store-room. Like Chapel Lane, it has been greatly altered and there has been some industrial usage, particularly by a firm making one of the brands of Kendal Mint Cake.

The building with the clock projecting over the street is the old Moot Hall which served as the Town Hall and Court of Justice for over 250 years before the Corporation moved to the new Town Hall. In 1969 the building was badly damaged by arson but has been tastefully rebuilt as a shop.

Right: As part of the celebration of Queen Victoria's Diamond Jubilee, Abbot Hall Park was bought by Kendal Corporation. A tea party and entertainment was given to the old people of the town, the men being given a present of tobacco and the women a cake. This fine gateway was the entrance through a wall around the park which has been the venue for a multitude of public events.

Below left: Dorothy Dowker left a sizeable legacy in 1831 to found the charitable Dowker's Hospital, an almshouse known locally as the Old Maids Hospital. The building, by George Webster, stood beside the path to Abbot Hall Park until it was demolished in 1963 to make a new road.

Below right: The hospital accommodated six poor, good and chaste women of Kendal who had reached the age of fifty without marrying – only women. The punning coat of arms on the front bore ducks – but no drakes! A dole is still paid to five elderly ladies in Kendal.

Above left: Near the corner of Captain French Lane stood the 150-year-old Bear and Ragged Staff Inn. Its sign referred to the arms of the Warwick family where a bear is seen chained to a wooden post. Arthgal, first Lord of Warwick, strangled a bear with his hands and Morvidius slew a giant with a club made from a tree. Shakespeare refers to the family in *Henry VI Part 2*.

Above right: The boundary between Kirkland and Market Kendal was Blind Beck, a stream running down from Kendal Fell to the river – that is when it is not waterless in dry weather! In the nineteenth century it became an open sewer, adding to the unhealthy nature of Kirkland. It now runs behind houses and passes under the old bridge beneath Kirkland. The name Blind comes from the old word blaen – town end.

Left: Collin Croft is one of the few Kendal yards relatively untouched by the wholesale demolition of the 1960s, the far end leading up through enclosed steps to Beast Banks. It contained a mixture of cottages and workshops and until 1850 an open drain ran down the centre. Its restoration by the Kendal Civic Society in 1980 earned a Civic Trust Award. A blacksmith still operates in the croft.

Above: Thomas Sandes, a wealthy cloth merchant and Mayor of Kendal, built Sandes Hospital almshouses in 1670 for eight poor widows. The Bluecoat School, built at the far end of the gardens, was amalgamated with Kendal Grammar School in 1889.

Right: The gatehouse bears the Sandes' arms and was the master's house and the first schoolroom and library. It is now a tea room. Miles Thompson rebuilt the cottages in 1852 into conventional almshouses. *Inset:* In the wall under the gatehouse arch is a box once used for receiving gifts or alms towards the upkeep of the inmates of the hospital, bearing the words, 'Remember the Poore'.

The Bank of Westmorland, with its fine Doric front and double staircase from the street, was designed by the Kendal architect George Webster. The bank moved into the building in 1835, the manager and his family living on the upper floor.

Five years later the lion couchant was added on the roof to indicate financial strength and probity. It is made of Coade Stone, an artificial stone produced in the nineteenth century on London's South Bank. A lion made of the same hard-wearing material stands today at the foot of Westminster Bridge in London.

Right: The first two banks in Kendal were opened by the Wakefields and the Crewdsons, both Quakers, on the same day, 1 January 1788. The two amalgamated in 1840 and became the Kendal Bank in this building. Its reputation was such that it was trusted above the Bank of England during the Napoleonic Wars in 1797. It was taken over in turn by the Bank of Liverpool, Martins Bank and Barclays.

Below: Bank notes were known as Promissory Notes as they bore the bank's words, 'Promise to Pay' – a guarantee of security.

Kendal loved to dress its streets to celebrate great occasions. Highgate is decorated for the coronation of Edward VII in 1902. The celebrations were postponed when he was stricken with appendicitis and the decorations taken down, to be replaced when the good news of his recovery was made public. Then the fun really began in Kendal.

Opposite above: The unusual width of the roadway opposite the Town Hall indicates where the Newbiggin stood from around 1500. It was a two-storey wooden building with a projecting upper storey. On the ground floor were shops, and animals were slaughtered in the street. There was only a narrow passage on each side producing a growing traffic and health hazard. The Corporation bought the building in 1803 and demolished it.

Opposite below: Francis Webster re-built the old Leaden or Leather Hall, a cloth exchange, in 1825 to form the White Hall which was used as assembly rooms containing a billiards room, news rooms, a lecture hall and a ballroom. When the Moot Hall was closed in 1849 this building was converted into a Town Hall with lock-up cells in the basement. The cupola was replaced by a clock tower in 1861.

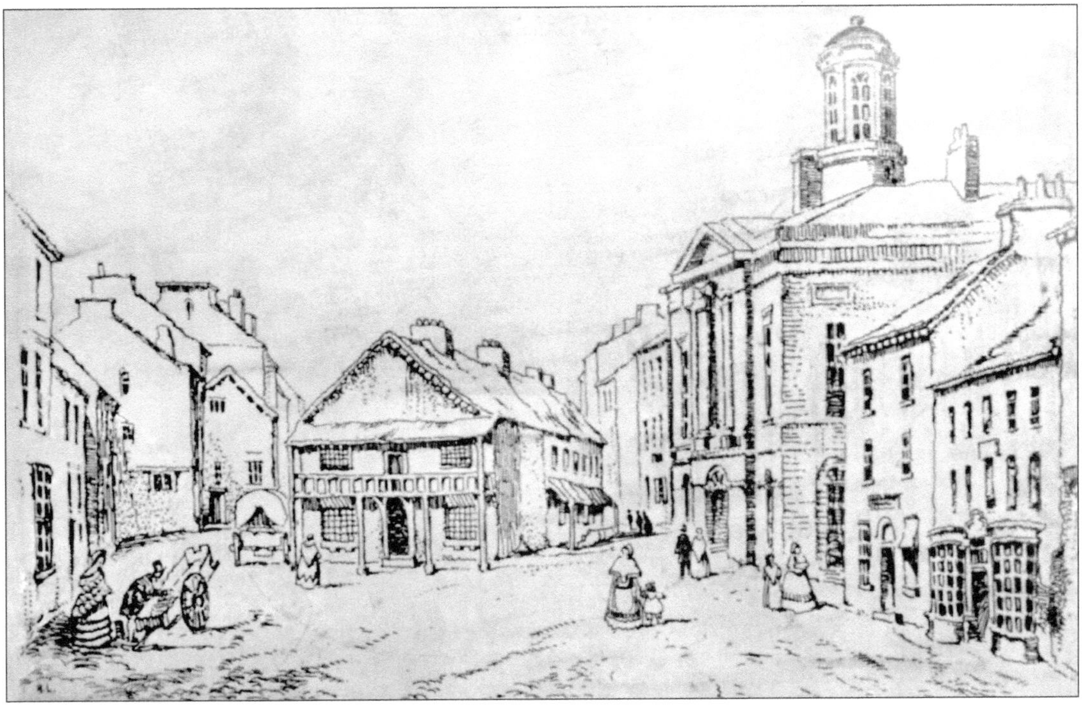

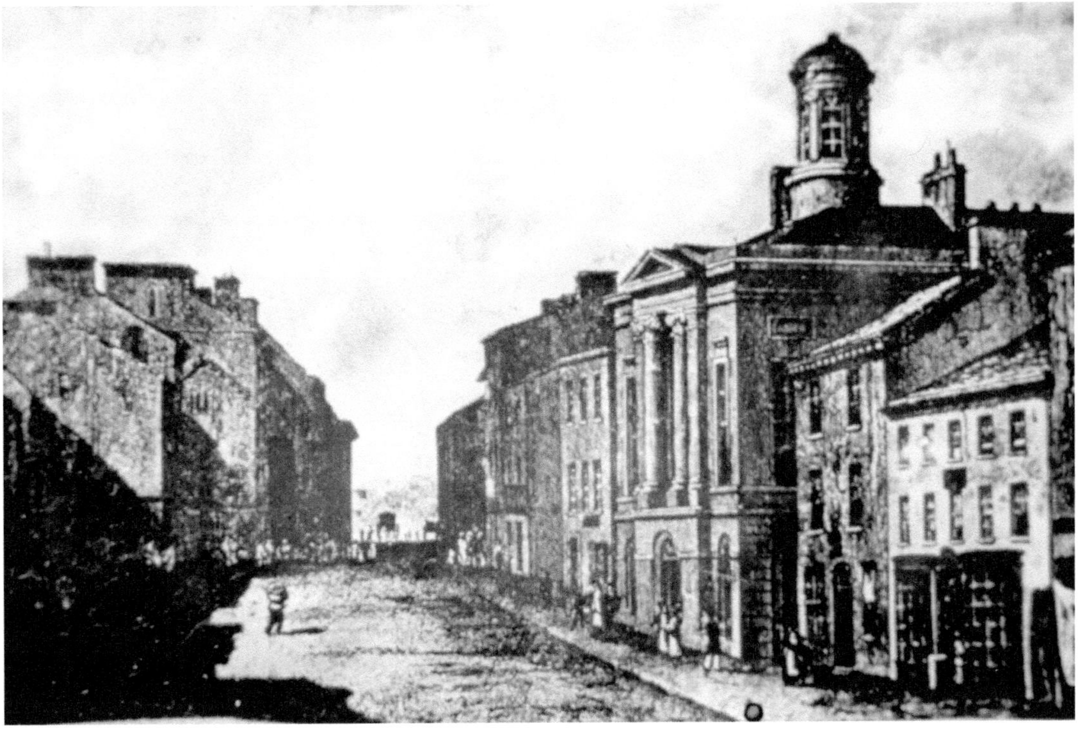

Above: Alderman and Mrs Bindloss were great benefactors to the town. He was Mayor of Kendal six times. A room in the Town Hall was named in his honour and below the clock face in the tower is a carved letter 'B' as a memorial to him. Mrs Bindloss set the new clock going at 11 o'clock on 22 June 1897 to start the Queen Victoria's Diamond Jubilee celebrations.

Left: The Town Hall is the centre of the town. A new clock tower replaced the old one, large enough to contain the eleven bells which strike the hours and quarters and play folk tunes from a carillon. Over the canopy above the entrance is carved the town coat of arms which can also be seen etched on the windows in the adjacent Lowther Street.

The shapeless lump of stone outside the Town Hall is of great historical importance. It is all that is left of the base of the ancient market cross from which public announcements and proclamations had been made for centuries, hence its name, the Call Stone. After 1765, when it presented a traffic obstruction in Stricklandgate, it was moved from place to place and eventually the remains found their present home.

The building beside the Town Hall was once the Angel Inn. On the roof between two sets of diamond chimneys is a small box-like construction which started life as a pigeoncote but by the eighteenth century had become a cockpit where contests between fighting birds took place. Cockfighting became illegal in 1849 but was still indulged there for a time under the very nose of the nearby police office.

The Commercial Hotel in Highgate was built in 1804 on the site of the earlier Royal Oak Hotel. Its sign was a bunch of grapes. In later years the Commercial became the Kendal Hotel and was popular with tourists. When that closed in the 1980s the ground floor was taken over by a building society.

In company with many yards in Kendal, Grove's Yard in Highgate was named after the principal resident, Richard Grove, who lived in a cottage there where he operated a dyeworks. The yard, the appearance of which is typical of Kendal's yards, was owned by Octavius Thompson and F. Robinson although they both lived elsewhere.

The Fleece Inn is Kendal's oldest surviving inn. It was probably built in 1656 and has a jetted upper floor. Its former title was the Golden Fleece Inn and its sign was the emblem of the Woolcombers which they carried in the guild processions. At one time the ground floor was used by a butcher when the windows were open to the air and closed by wooden shutters at night.

William Cock, a mercer and Mayor of Kendal in 1692, lived on the south side of Cock Lane, named after him, which became Fleece Inn Yard. His house was used for a time by the Golden Fleece Inn to accommodate the humbler guests who arrived by public coach. It later became a seedman's shop.

Above: The 1960s were a time of great change in Kendal. The grey days of war were past and minds were trained to a new future. The yards between Highgate and the river were considered insanitary and below the standard then required. Wholesale demolition ensued.

James Meldrum set up a nursery behind the Woolpack Inn in 1810. Some years later it was bought by Clarence Webb who grew flowers and vegetables and held an annual show of home-grown onions. He propagated new varieties including the famous 'Webb's Wonderful Lettuce'. In the 1960s the nursery was moved to a new site in Burneside Road.

Right: Leading from Webb's nurseries to the river was a stone-built culvert which helped to drain the area of excessive water after heavy rain. This was one of a number of similar culverts leading from the rising ground of Fellside, all of which, being underground, were never noticed by the general public and sometimes even by modern civil engineers.

Opposite below: With a clear space and high hopes, modern blocks of housing were erected along Waterside, which now had a more open aspect over the river to Castle Hill, and some of the old yard names were retained where appropriate. The housing was given a congratulatory national award for their design.

The Rose and Crown and White Lion Inns stood side by side in Stricklandgate. The White Lion was a very ancient posting inn, first mentioned in 1697. It had a bowling green and, later, a famed dancing room. When workmen were altering a wall in the inn they found a shearman's token for a farthing dated 1666, something that tradesmen used for currency at that time.

The first stagecoach ran from the King's Arms Inn in Stricklandgate twice a week from 1763. Called the Flying Machine, it reached London in three days. The inn became the leading hostelry in the town and was famed for its food, especially potted char and hotpot. In 1841 it served a pie weighing seventy-eight pounds in a dish 7ft round.

Above left: The King's Arms was a straggling old inn with two galleries leading to the bedrooms. On the ground floor were shops and a coach booking office with the usual yard separating it from the adjacent properties.

Above right: Edward Woof is the man seen in the yard. He was the hotel porter until the closure of the King's Arms in 1934. When he retired, Lord Lonsdale initiated a collection for him and he was presented with a gold watch and chain.

There was a thriving business in transporting guests to and from the hotels in the town as well as general use as a taxi. Anthony Thornbarrow was kept busy performing such duties. His two-horse conveyance is seen outside the King's Arms Hotel. The Moot Hall is on the right, mid-distance.

When one of the cottages in the Elephant Inn yard off Stricklandgate was demolished around 1959 some fine oak panelling was found in the parlour bearing the initials T.K.S. of Thomas Sandes and his wife Katherine and the date 1651. It is preserved in the Museum of Lakeland Life and Industry. This fine staircase led to the upper floor.

Justice Thomas Shepherd provided hospitality to Bonnie Prince Charlie in his house at the northern end of Stricklandgate on his return from defeat at Derby in 1745. Refreshed, the prince went on his way with the remnants of his army, followed in hot pursuit by the Duke of Cumberland who also spent the night at the house, in the very bed that the prince had graced.

Strickland House was the dower house of the Strickland family. John Strickland, lead merchant and Mayor of Kendal in 1717, lived there. His initials and that of his wife, Frances, were seen on a leaden spout together with the date 1711 when the house was probably rebuilt. It has since been demolished.

The Working Mens' Institute, tucked into the corner of the Market Place, has had a varied life. In the seventeenth century it was a wool weigh loft and a poultry market, later becoming a theatre and then a church. The Wesleyan Stephen Brunskill preached from the roofed balcony on the left. It became a library and newsroom for working men, a testimonial to the Victorians' eagerness for education and self-help.

Above left and right: The Woolpack was one of Kendal's oldest inns and was rebuilt in 1781, catering mainly for carriers. The yard behind contains a building that has been in turn a church, dancing school, soup kitchen and an industrial school. The high, wide arch at its side is a reminder of the lumbering wagons piled high with bales of wool that made their way to the warehouses and stables at the rear of the yard.

Right: The Globe Inn in the Market Place dates from the seventeenth century and is one of Kendal's few remaining lath and plaster houses with overhanging upper storeys. After a fire in 1968 it was rebuilt and restored. The name 'globe' is a reminder of the mercers (silk merchants), after whom a lane on that side of the Market Place was named. The public stocks stood outside the front door until 1835.

Below: When the Globe Inn was being rebuilt an ancient well was found at the rear. This would have supplied the water used in the kitchen and for the guests in their rooms. It might also have been used in brewing. Many old inns brewed their own beer. By 1855 the inn had become more of a drinking house for the lower classes.

Left: Police Office Yard, linking Finkle Street with the Market Place, afforded entry to the town's police station. The Borough Police Force was established in 1835 and reorganised in 1844. The police administered the fire brigade with a fire station, built alongside the police office in Finkle Street in 1838, which has for long been shops.

Below: The New Shambles, formerly Watt Lane, between Finkle Street and the Market Place, was opened in 1804. The Shambles is the place where butchers operated and where animals were slaughtered outside, the blood and waste material being collected in the centre to be carried or drained away. The New Shambles replaced the Old Shambles off Highgate and was closed when a town abattoir was opened at Canal Head.

Right: The Chocolate Shop at the foot of Branthwaite Brow is certainly seventeenth century but don't be fooled by the date 1657 on its sign. That is the year when the first chocolate shop was opened in England, in Bishopsgate in London. Branthwaite Brow still sports a cobbled roadway, which helped carthorses struggling to haul their heavy carts up into the Market Place.

Below: Branthwaite Brow was originally very narrow and in 1850, after many years of deliberation, the local Board of Health decided to widen it. This involved the demolition of houses, mainly on the west side. When a row of shops was built there an innovative plan was conceived to face them with cast-iron plates. This was completed in 1853 as the date on the frontage shows.

Above: Sandes Avenue was opened in 1887 as a new road from the north of the town to the railway station and, incidentally, supplemented and to some extent replaced Finkle Street and Stramongate in their role as the road to Scotland. It was a fine, wide, tree-lined thoroughfare lined with houses, industrial premises and the Friends School playing field. It has now been altered almost beyond recognition.

Left: Entry Lane is an ancient pathway leading from Fellside down to the Market Place. Of course, it has been much altered over the centuries but in places it still emanates a feeling of the past when it was trod by our ancestors.

Above: The top part of Stramongate opens out into a wide thoroughfare which was so designed to accommodate market stalls on each side on the weekly market days. It is another very ancient road, part of the road to Scotland, and used to be a street of inns, now mostly gone as the need for them has passed.

Right: The Dun Horse was one of the old inns in Stramongate, its yard stretching down towards New Road. It had an almost unique enclosed corridor over the yard joining the two sides of the building. In 1832 it was described as a middle-class inn with three drinking rooms, five bedrooms, a large dining room and stabling for fourteen horses. It is now a public house.

A number of prominent Westmorland families had a town house in Kendal. The Bellingham's house in Stramongate was built in 1544. The date tablet on the gable was placed there when the house was rebuilt in 1863, the façade being hardly changed. The house has been used as a shop for many years. In the yard at the side is an old pump and tethering ring used when watering horses.

On the side of the ancient cross house at the entrance to the Friends Meeting House in Stramongate is the finest example in Kendal of a Westmorland long-case window. To avoid paying tax, windows were incorporated, lighting more than one floor. This is 33ft tall and less than 3ft wide with ninety-nine panes of glass giving light to all the floors of the house.

Above: Castle Dairy is Kendal's oldest building, continuously occupied since at least the fourteenth century, being contemporary with Kendal Castle for which it was probably a dower house and not a dairy. It was refurbished by Anthony Garnett in 1564 who transformed it into an Elizabethan dwelling-house. On the gables fronting the street are signs of old dovecotes.

Right: Much of the interior of the Castle Dairy remains as it was 400 years ago. In a bedroom is a large sixteenth-century carved tester bed. Bosses in the room bear the Parr family coat of arms and the windows have four diamond-shaped panes decorated with dates, pictures and words. It is said that the room might once have been used as a chapel

Above: The Norse word *finkle* for 'elbow' aptly describes the shape of Finkle Street. Another meaning is 'rubbish heap' and this could have portrayed the state of the fish market at the Highgate end before it was moved to the Market Place. The area was improved to create an open space for public events where an open-roofed platform, the Birdcage, now stands. It is seen decorated for George V's coronation.

Left: Seen here from the Stramongate end, it is difficult now to imagine that the present pedestrianised Finkle Street was once filled with two-way traffic. The van is a Ford T-type. It was widened only in parts and a new road was built parallel to it towards the river. That road eventually became redundant and Finkle Street is now the haunt of tourists and shoppers.

Above: Opposite the Town Hall, Allhallows Lane begins the packhorse trade route to Ulverston and Whitehaven. It was named after the medieval chapel of the Holy Cross and Allhallows, situated near to the foot of Beast Banks, which closed during the Reformation. The building on the right was once the Dolphin Inn. On the left is Cartmell's fent shop before it was demolished when the lane was widened in 1914.

Right: Fellside had grown without planning for centuries. It was a self-contained community and people would come out into the lanes and ginnels to gossip or exchange news and views. For the younger children these were their playgrounds. The older ones were expected to work to help the family income as soon as they were old enough, often before the age of ten.

Left: The inhabitants of Fellside, like those here in Fountain Brow, were generally poor labouring families, many of them engaged in one or other part of the woollen industry. Looms were worked in cottages and the dust and wool fibres filled the air, causing dry and inflamed throats. Visits to the public house became a popular necessity where the cares of the day could be washed into an alcoholic unconsciousness.

Below: The name T-Well is a corruption of the common expression, 't'well' meaning, 'the well'. The T-Well was Fellside's main water supply and became a place where housewives met to share small talk and grumbles. It was often said that the water there made the best cup of tea in Kendal. However, it became dirty and germ-ridden, causing illnesses like cholera that plagued Fellsiders, especially the children.

Syke Lane was a steep, cobbled lane leading from Fountain Brow to Low Fellside above the town. It was lined with cottages set at odd angles with doors opening directly on to the lane. It was once the worst plague spot in the town, with a heavily polluted drain or open sewer flowing down it. Almost the whole of Fellside was demolished in the 1960s to create a characterless housing development.

Far Cross Bank is the eastern extremity of the town where the roads to Shap and Appleby divide. It used to be a vibrant community of poorer labouring families. The last thatched cottage in Kendal was pulled down there in 1815. Although somewhat of a slum, it did have redeeming features. One little girl liked to visit her grandma there as she had a chain to pull in the lavatory!

THE MANAGERS OF ·THE

CASTLE STREET SCHOOL

Inform the Parents of their Scholars that from the
1st of November their Terms will be as follows:—

Infants (as at present) ...   ...   2*d*. weekly.
Children in Standards I, II, & III   3*d*. „
In Standards IV, V, & VI   ...   4*d*. „

The Managers make this advance in con-
sequence of the increased Expense of the School,
owing to the number of Teachers now required
by Government.

The present Rate of School-pence does not
meet HALF of the Annual Expenses of the School.

Kendal, Oct. 15th, 1875.

Above left: Castle Street British Girls' and Infants' School was an important part of Kendal's history. It was opened in 1830 by Quakers 'for the education of the labouring and manufacturing classes of society of every religious persuasion'. Miss Elizabeth Herriott was the first mistress, and girls as young as thirteen became pupil teachers to help her.

Above right: The children paid a few pence a week for their education.

The school was rebuilt in 1899, the year when the girls' choir came first in the Mary Wakefield Musical Festival. In the 1930s it became a public elementary junior mixed school; it closed in 1968 and in the 1990s a house was built on the site, named appropriately School House.

In contrast to the poorer areas of Kendal, pleasant houses and villas were built on the outskirts of the town. One such place was Greenside, high above Beast Banks. Around 1870 the local architect Stephen Shaw designed fine terraced houses for the better-off where they could live in the clean air and enjoy the sylvan views.

The Duke of Cumberland public house is on the road junction at Far Cross Bank. It is named after the duke, nicknamed 'The Butcher', who chased Bonnie Prince Charlie over the border in 1745. It is said that he stopped at the inn on his way. An old character named Jack Wharton, a mole catcher from Shap, was remembered for years by his chair kept in his place in the bar.

John Sleddall was a descendant of Thomas Sleddall, Mayor of Kendal in 1636. He intended to build almshouses at New Hutton in celebration of Queen Victoria's Golden Jubilee and set up a foundation for the purpose. It is said that when he called on the vicar to discuss the project, he was kept waiting in a draughty corridor and left in a huff, building them instead on Aynam Road in Kendal.

The Kendal Fell Trust established the town Poor House in 1769 where men and women were kept separate and had to earn their own keep. The diet was very basic and the beds were searched each morning for fleas. Taken over by the Poor Law Union in 1836 as a workhouse, it served that purpose until no longer needed when it became a geriatric hospital, later demolished for housing.

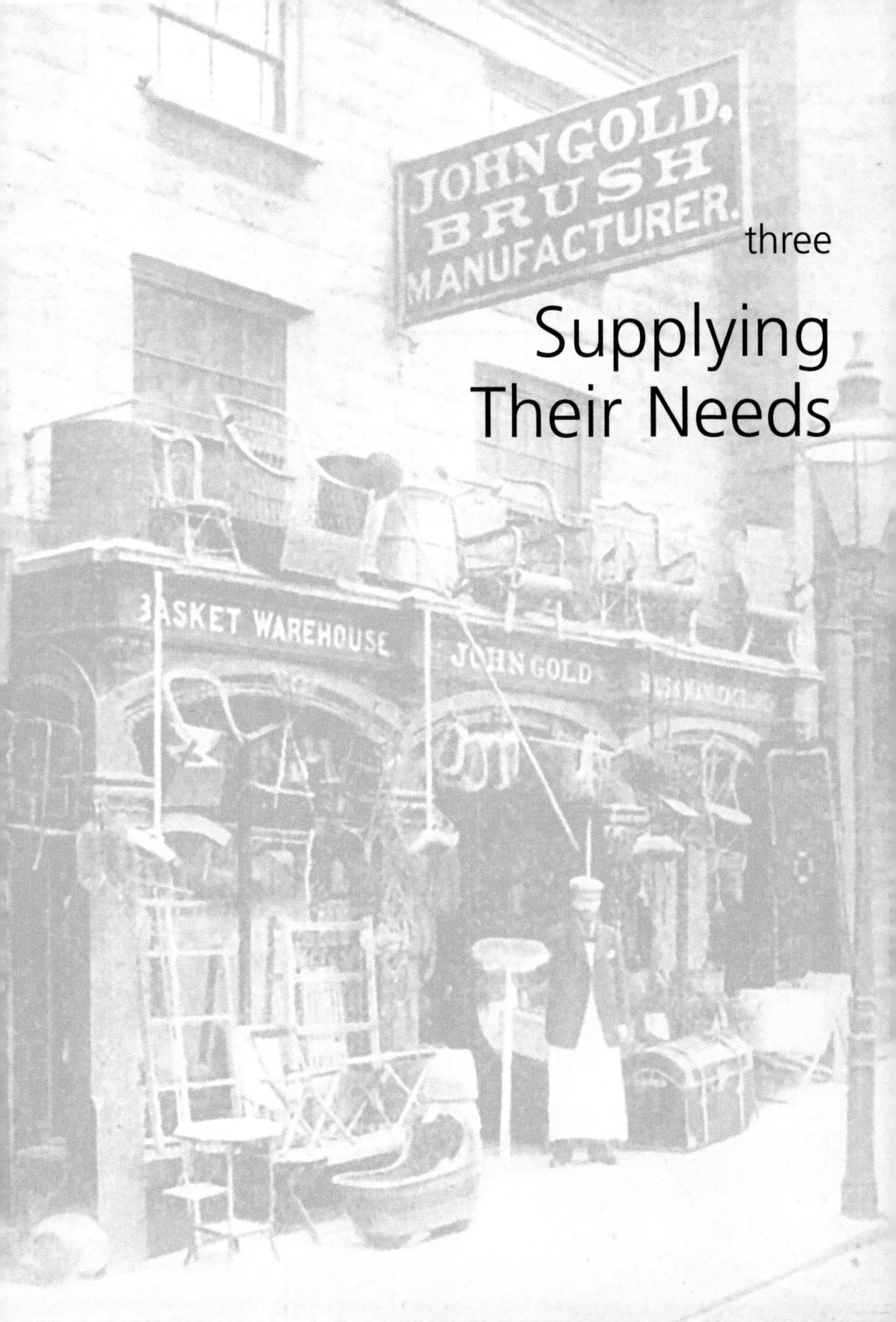

JOHN GOLD, BRUSH MANUFACTURER.

three

Supplying Their Needs

BASKET WAREHOUSE

JOHN GOLD

Being a market town, Kendal was plentifully supplied with shops and other suppliers of all needs. Inhabitants of the towns and villages from a wide area around would descend on the town, especially on the market days of Wednesday and Saturday when it would be filled with people shopping and meeting friends for the weekly 'crack'. Farmers and housewives would bring their produce there for sale and much bargaining and bartering would go on so that all would return home satisfied, their needs replenished for another week. The Market Place is still the locale for this as it has been for centuries, despite the changes it has endured.

The main streets are still lined with shops of all kinds, some still trading after nearly a century, many of them in buildings that have seen only minor changes. The streets were also the sites of markets selling specific goods like fish and seasonal kinds like fruit.

Those coming to the town from a distance required accommodation for themselves and stabling for their horses as well as food and liquid refreshment. The many inns and public houses, some still standing, provided this service and hotels catered for those requiring superior and longer stays.

The Hen Market in Stramongate is typical of places in the town where traders brought their goods for sale on the roadside stalls. Annual poultry shows were held in the Market Hall each autumn.

Above: For centuries meat was butchered and sold from open stalls set up in front of places like the Butchers Rows on each side of Highgate from Finkle Street to Allhallows Lane. In 1785 they were displaced by the Old Shambles which contained cottages, some forty shops and the Butchers Arms public house. This area became the site of the Kendal Bank.

Right: Titus Wilson's old shop was built in Elizabethan times, its galleried front being altered by the Kendal architect, Webster, in 1820. It later became a shop. Wilson bought it around 1850 and it was the first shop in Kendal to have electric light. According to legend, an earlier occupier, Thomas Hudson, nailed the first penny he earned to a beam for good luck – and it seemed to work!

Above: The name of Quiggin is synonymous with Kendal Mint Cake which the firm is still making after over 160 years. Their shop in Stricklandgate, on the corner of Library Road, now houses an optician. Horse transport, redolent of a slower pace of life, has given way to the ubiquitous motor.

Left: John Gold, a close competitor of Rainforth Hodgson, stands in front of his shop and brush factory in Stricklandgate. As was common with shopkeepers in the nineteenth century he displayed as much of his stock as possible for potential purchasers to view, even though it spilled out on to the street.

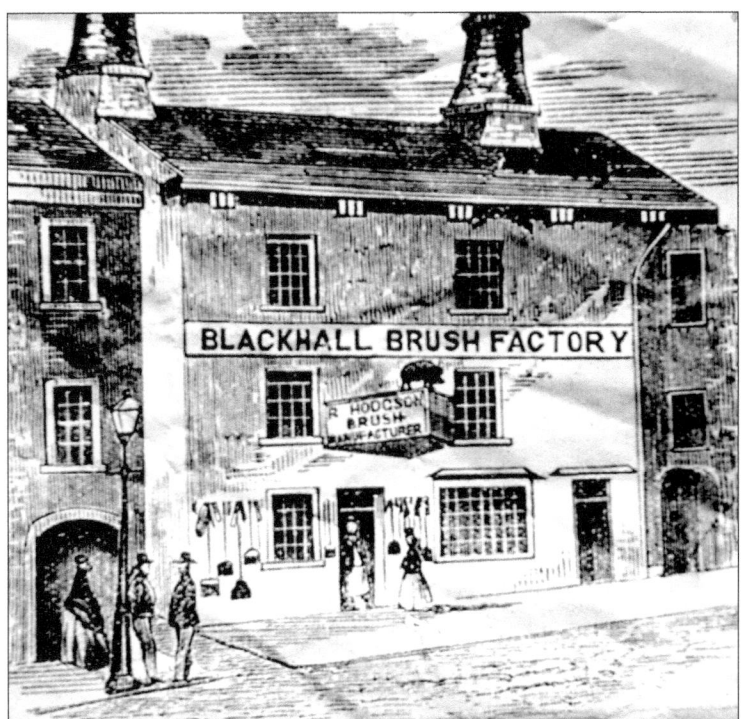

Black Hall in Stricklandgate was originally the house of Kendal's first mayor in 1575. It became Rainforth Hodgson's brush factory in 1838 and now houses an estate agent.

Inn and tradesmens' signs were essential in days before universal literacy to inform people what business was being carried out. The life-sized model of the Bristly Hog, whose back was decorated with bristles, was mounted over the front of the Black Hall Brush Factory.

Left: Waterloo House in Finkle Street was the drapery shop of E. & C. Dawson. In 1862 the Kendal Co-operative Society was founded and took over the premises which was the first shop in Kendal with large plate-glass windows. With deteriorating trading conditions the shop was closed around 1960 and a supermarket was opened in Stricklandgate which struggled on until 1989.

Below: The family run corner shop is no modern phenomenon. At the top of Beast Banks, on the corner of Belmont, the Dixon family had a grocery and provisions shop. It might be Mrs Dixon herself standing in the doorway. In later years the shop became a bacon wholesaler's and then a confectioner's and finally was incorporated into the house beside it.

Many houses along the streets in Kendal were built without any standard plan. In 1769 it was said of them that they were 'standing back to back, corner to corner … without intent or meaning.' Sedgwick's, the butchers in Highgate next to Jennings'Yard, is one such, projecting into the street quite out of line with the others. It is now an office.

Fleet's grocers shop in Allhallows Lane was typical of the small, family owned, independent shops which stood their ground against the growing competition from the larger national firms. Standing outside are, from the left: Jim Graham the errand boy with his bicycle, Mr Fleet, - ? -, Mrs Fleet, Mabel ?.

Above: Robert and Thomas Thompson were members of an extensive local family. Having served their time with Mr Blacow, the brothers set up as gentlemen's outfitters in Finkle Street where children at the high and grammar schools had to buy their school uniforms. Robert was a Dickensian character who walked through the Market Place each morning wearing spats and replying to greetings with, 'Good morning boys.' This is now a toy shop.

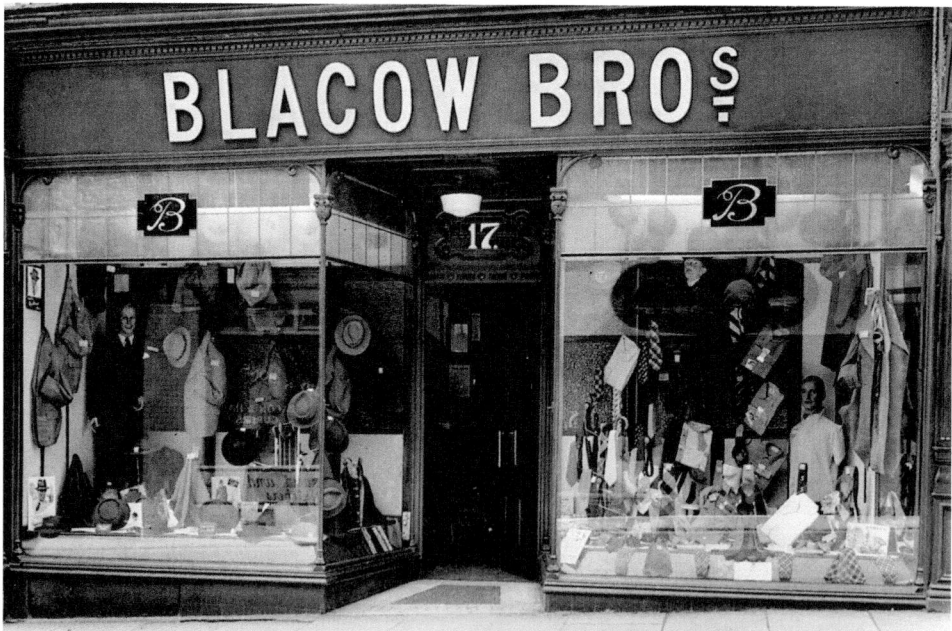

QUALITY . . .
and
PRICE . . . . .

considered, we offer easily the
best value in Artificial Teeth
to-day.
Compare the Quality of . . .

Park & Co.'s

with the best Teeth you know of;
you will not be disappointed.
Judge Quality only by results;
this done we will take our
chances.

Teeth were a problem from childhood to the grave before improvements were made in dental hygiene and treatment. Preparations were advertised for soothing teething infants, and others like Nervine, relieved toothache and itching teeth in adults. Teeth could be removed to solve problems but toothless gums were not acceptable to fashionable women. Park & Co. advertised their artificial teeth as a desirable aid to beauty and they became all the rage.

Above: John Monkhouse was a well-known businessman and a passionate councillor. He became mayor three times, in 1896, 1902 and 1903. He was also a prominent member of the Fire Engine Committee. In business he was a successful auctioneer, selling many important properties in the town.

Opposite below: Blacow Brothers have traded in Kendal for over 200 years. The family business was established in Finkle Street in 1772, trading there as hatters, hosiers and tailors until 2005 when it relocated to the new Elephant Yard shopping mall.

Opposite: Joseph Hunter provided a valuable service to the poorer people of Kendal in buying and selling second-hand furniture at his shop in Stramongate.

Left: Henry Roberts came from Lancaster in 1890 and opened a bookshop in St George's buildings. In 1903 he moved his shop to the top of Finkle Street where it thrived. He died in the 1950s and the shop was carried on by his daughter.

Below: When the lease expired in 1985 the shop, now owned by a large company, moved to the historic Bellingham House at the top of Stramongate.

George Stubbs was a well-respected tailor whose shop stood on the corner of Stricklandgate and Sandes Avenue where he was in business for about forty years. Although partially disabled, he was an active bowler and was a founder and director of the Victoria Bowling Club. The spinneret on the tower surmounting his shop became unsafe in the 1960s and had to be taken down before it fell and injured someone.

Most of the shops in the town specialised in particular products. Bailie & Hargreaves were ironmongers selling a wide variety from fire irons and coal vases to teapots, cutlery, iron bedsteads, kitchen ranges, paraffin and petrol for lamps. They were local agents for 'Encore' cut-throat razors and the tortoise stove.

Right: Alfred Heap, chemist and optician, had a grand shop at the top of Finkle Street, built in bricks of an apricot colour. The girls looking out of the window are his daughters Doris and her sister. Inside the shop a bright coke fire was kept burning in a large black stove. Alfred made his own sheep dip which he supplied to many local landowners, including the Bagots of Levens Hall.

Below: In the later eighteenth century, mail coaches collected letters from the King's Arms posting inn. In 1800 there was a post office in Highgate and, after a number of moves, it settled in 1877 in Central Buildings in Finkle Street. In 1930 a purpose-built post office was constructed on the site of the old Strickland dower house where it remains today.

Left: Thomas and Edmund Rhodes had a shop in Highgate from 1854 selling clocks and watches. In days when few working men carried watches, the large clock on the wall, together with that on the Town Hall, showed Greenwich Mean Time. Their advertisement of 1909 showed that the cheapest pocket watch cost 12s 6d, a large amount of money for a labourer. Thomas died and the firm was sold in 1936.

Below: The War Office lent the Corporation an old 18-pounder gun from HMS *Warspite* of 1807. As a Time Gun, mounted in Serpentine Woods and fired by electricity from Rhodes' shop, it indicated 1 p.m. each day from 6 September 1873. When it wore out it was placed on a carriage and displayed in Abbot Hall Park. It was taken for wartime scrap and its replacement mysteriously disappeared in 1940.

The hotel on the eastern end of Wildman Street was the Lowther Arms. When the railway came in 1846, with the station opposite, it was renamed the Railway Hotel. It was then known as the Railway & Commercial Hotel, the Railway and County Hotel, and finally the County Hotel, keeping up with the changing demands of the times. In the 1960s it gained the reputation of being the acknowledged primary venue for social gatherings.

The Horse and Rainbow Inn opened in the seventeenth century. The date 1638 was found during rebuilding. It had no sign until 1856, being known until then just as William and Elinor Lawn's. The new landlord, James Harker, set up the sign of a rainbow arching over a crouching black horse. As an hotel it catered for a superior class of clientele and had a dining room which could seat fifty.

Above: Fish was sold at the top of Finkle Street for 200 years or more, the smell being kept well away from the Market Place. Up to the 1960s most of the fish sold at the Saturday market came from the Lakes or the nearby sea estuary. The market was moved into the Market Place in 1927. The man in the bowler hat is Mr McIntyre, a scissors grinder.

Left: Fruit of every kind was displayed for sale from boxes, stalls and carts along the roadside in Highgate on market days. Plum Saturday each autumn brought damsons from the nearby Lyth Valley. On one occasion carts arrived at 3 a.m. and lined one side of the road stretching for half a mile. Because of increased traffic in Highgate the fruit market was moved to the Market Place in 1926.

Above: The Charter of AD 1189 established a weekly Saturday market to be held in the Market Place which was more extensive in area then. A Wednesday market was added in the nineteenth century and these two market days saw the place filled with stalls with crowds of people from the town and surrounding villages seeking the best bargains. It is still busy on market days and holds a monthly farmers' market.

Right: The Market Place was the host to regular fairs specialising in particular products. These were held at the same times each year according to the season.

KENDAL
WOOL & CHEESE
FAIR.

ESTABLISHED   IN THE YEAR 1852.

Kendal, July 15th, 1854.

Notice is hereby given.

That the **FIRST FAIR** for the present year will be held in the **MARKET PLACE**, **KENDAL**, on *Tuesday, the 8th of August,* and the **SECOND** on *Tuesday, the 5th of September,* (being the Kendal Fortnight Fat Fairs), at 1 o'clock in the afternoon.

☞ In future years the Fair will be held on the first Fortnight Fair in August and September, or on such days as may be agreed upon by the Committee

COMMITTEE:

WILLIAM TALBOT,	THOMAS WALKER,	WILLIAM ELLISON, Jun.
JOHN DENNISON,	ROBERT HARRISON,	JAMES DIXON,
JOSEPH MORTON,	WILLIAM SIMPSON,	ROBERT FENTON,
JOHN WATSON,	JOSEPH BENN, Jun.,	EDWARD MARTINDALE.
	ROWLAND PARKER,	

WILLIAM ELLISON, Chairman.

J. DAWSON, PRINTER, KENDAL.

The indoor Market Hall opened in 1887 celebrating the Queen's Golden Jubilee. Market tolls were abolished in 1864. When the district council took over in 1974 it attempted, fairly successfully, to break the ancient tradition of Kendalians being allowed to trade in the Market Hall free of charge. Today, even after the hall has become part of a shopping mall, a few local people still trade there.

The ancient town well existed at the top of Finkle Street from before 1594. Some 250 years later, in 1856, a drinking fountain was placed in Crock Lane, beside the Pump Inn, much to the delight of small boys. When the inn was demolished the fountain was moved in 1883 to Aynam Road where it stands today dry and disused, still bearing the date 1857 – no-one bothered to correct it!

four

Industry and Transport

Kendal in the nineteenth century was a busy town, being in many ways self-sufficient with a host of workshops, large and small, catering for its several needs. Along its river were mills, tanneries and wool manufactories, all casting their waste into it while, in return, it provided power for them. The river has always been both a blessing and a bane. It required bridges to take its roads across it. It is fast-flowing yet shallow, causing regular, ruinous flooding until the preventative work carried out in the 1970s. Even now the waters can overlap the banks, fortunately without the dire results previously endured. From early days the horse was the main beast of burden and means of transport. The canal and railway served the town well but both were superseded by the motor vehicle as the main means of transport.

Manufacturing woollens, notably the tweed for which Kendal was famous, Braithwaite's Mill, set up by George Foster Braithwaite in the 1880s, was typical of the many mills along the river Kent. Dust, fibres and heat were a recipe for the outbreak of fires in mills, some of which became disastrous conflagrations. Braithwaite's Mill fortunately escaped serious fires.

The massive Bridge Mill, built in 1859, was one of the many that originally drew power from the river. Its length was necessary for drawing wire from blocks of metal to make cards for separating woollen fibres for spinning.

In later years it became a factory for knitting stockings and then for processing leather and cloth. At the end of the twentieth century it closed and was sympathetically rebuilt into offices.

Harold Day established a foundry in the Lound in 1850. In 1892 a new building was constructed at Canal Head. Known as Castle Foundry, it produced a wide range of products from grates and boilers to taps and milestones.

Gilbert Gilkes took over the foundry producing heavy ironwork, including the girders for Victoria Bridge and canal bridges, and became famous for making turbines. The foundry still operates as Gilbert Gilkes & Gordon.

Thomas Wilson opened a factory by the river in 1825 making fancy waistcoats. In 1843, Robert Somervell rented one of the buildings to set up a business that led to the famous K-Shoes which was once one of Kendal's leading employers. After being taken over by the Clarks Group in 1987, the factory went into decline and closed after nearly 175 years of shoemaking.

The Kendal-Lancaster Canal ended in the town with a large basin at Canal Head where barges were turned, loaded and unloaded. Industrial buildings grew up around the basin including the Castle Foundry and Iron Works, coal merchants, a stone works and the town's abattoir.

Kendal's gasworks were completed in 1825 alongside the canal by Parkside Road Bridge. An ascent by gas-filled balloon in that year was a popular event. The works were enlarged as the town's need for gas increased and closed in the 1960s with the introduction of natural gas. The gasholders, a local landmark, were removed some years later. The façade of the gas meter house is preserved at Abbot Hall.

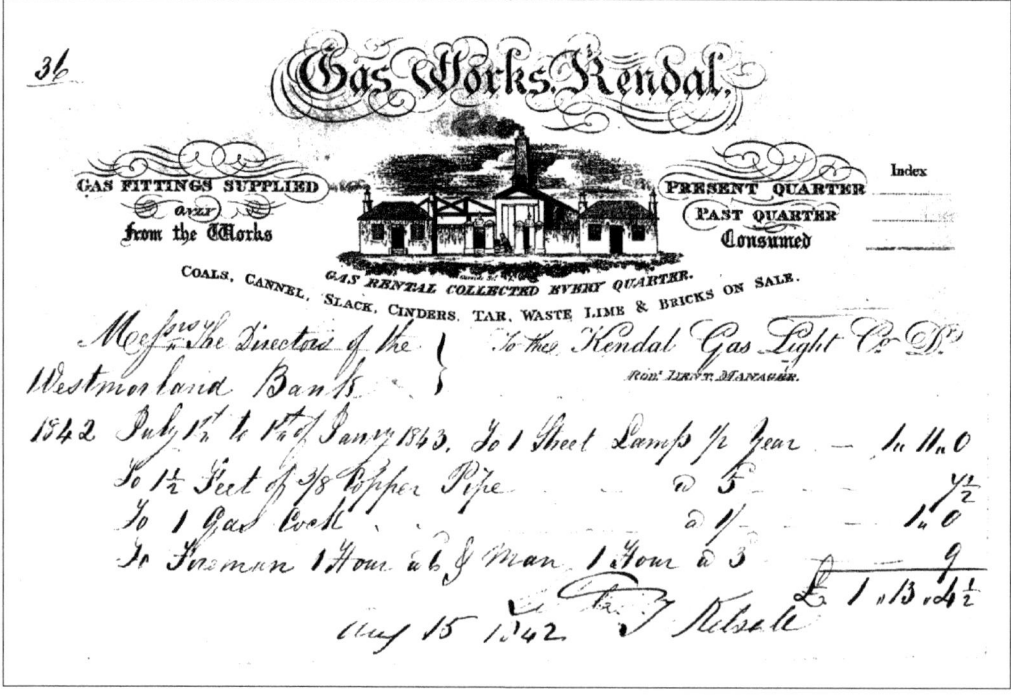

Founded in Kirkland in 1829, Wilkinson's became the foremost organ builders in the country, introducing many innovative ideas. In 1886 the works moved from Stramongate to a new purpose-built factory on Aynam Road. The Northern Counties Organ Manufactory, as it was named, was a family run business until amalgamated with Rushworth & Draper of Liverpool in 1957. It closed down in 1968 and the factory was converted into flats.

Kendal has been famous for snuff made from American tobacco since the seventeenth century. In 1841 John Thomas Illingworth joined the old established snuff maker, Samuel Gawith, and in 1867 left to set up his own company. When he died his sons carried it on. In 1920 the work was moved to Aynam Mills. That factory was burnt out in 1983 and the firm closed down three years later.

Opposite above: Low Mills began in 1826 as Winder's iron foundry. Then for fifty years it was in turn a woollen mill, a horse clothing factory, a comb mill and a snuff mill, becoming again a woollen manufactory and yarn spinners in 1905. It closed in the 1930s and the weir in the river forming a mill dam was removed. In 1937 the site was purchased for public walks and pleasure grounds.

Left: Kendal cottons – coarse woollen cloth – were woven, not only in the weaving shed and mills, but also in a vibrant cottage industry. Thread was spun from raw wool in galleries in the yards and weavers in the yards and on Fellside produced the cloth. This was taken to the river for washing and was placed on tenter frames on open land to dry and stretch.

Below: Robert Dixon worked at his hand loom in Yard 123 off Highgate for many years into the twentieth century.

Dick Ashburner was the last in a long line of blacksmiths who had worked in a forge in Elephant Yard for centuries. Some might well have shod packhorses in earlier days. Dick's motto was: 'By hammer and hand all things do stand.' During the development of the yard, the smithy was demolished and the contents sold, closing the door on a long succession of craftsmen.

YARD 48, HIGHGATE, KENDAL.

The Shoeing Forge, Collin Croft,
KENDAL.

E. T. DENNISON,

Begs to inform the Public that he is carrying on the business of Shoeing Smith at the above address, and hopes by strict attention to business, to merit a share of their patronage,

NOTE THE ADDRESS:

Horse Shoeing Forge, Collin Croft,
Highgate, Kendal.

ESTABLISHED 1897.

Above: Ernest T. Dennison opened his shoeing forge in Collin Croft in 1897 and lived almost on the job in a cottage behind the smithy at the Highgate end of the croft. Horses being in abundance at that time, his business thrived until the motor car took over.

Left: Advertising was most polite and unaggressive in days gone by.

Posed for their photograph in the coal yard, Harry Tidey is holding the yard dog and George Dennison is standing hatless on the right of the group. Coal was an important fuel for both cooking and domestic heating as well as in the factories.

George Dennison was the manager of the Beezon Road Coal Yard adjacent to the railway station. He is seen with Duke, one of the horses used to haul carts around the town delivering coal.

Above: As well as serving its commercial purpose, the Kendal-Lancaster Canal afforded pleasant walks along its towpath, sheltered in places by lines of trees planted along its banks. The fly-boats had ceased to run long before this photograph was taken but the barges still carried heavy goods until the closure of the canal around 1955 after which it was filled in and converted into a footpath.

Left: The haulage of freight by barge continued for many years after the railway bought the canal. William Vickers occupied his coal office at the beginning of the towpath at Canal Head where he dealt in bricks, hay and straw, all commodities suited to conveyance by the commodious barges and the slow pace of the canal.

The canal was used for many recreational purposes and there were complaints about men and boys bathing naked and affronting the sensitivities of ladies. Angling was another popular pastime. Men often fell into the canal when drunk and young women in trouble used it for committing suicide. This man is concentrating on his craft by the Highgate Settlings Bridge under Burton Road. The bridge is still there although completely buried.

Highlights of the children's year were the Sunday school and Whitsun excursions to Levens Park where they played games and enjoyed an alfresco tea party. Marching from the Sunday school to Canal Head to the music of a band they were taken, singing hymns, in coal barges which had been suitably scrubbed and fitted with forms from the school.

The bicycle craze hit Kendal towards the end of the nineteenth century and models of many different kinds could be seen in the streets and parades. The ungainly Ordinary was nicknamed the Penny Farthing because of its very differently sized wheels. It needed a courageous and athletic rider, like Mr Inman here, who was unafraid of spills. It was certainly not a bicycle for women.

The Safety Bicycle could be ridden with safety by both men and women and became the standard for the future. It was very popular and liberated both rich and poor to explore the countryside for recreation as well as for personal transportation and work. Carriers were fitted for errand boys to transport small goods. This man has found a novel way of hauling his charge.

Stramongate Bridge was of a typical medieval design with steep slopes on each side, causing problems to horses hauling heavy carts across it. St William's chantry chapel was built at the eastern end. In 1794 it was widened on each side instead of being rebuilt as it had been so strongly constructed that it could not be taken down even with excessive blasting.

Water from the river was diverted through mill races to power mills. This one was for Castle Mill which is thought to have been built on the site of Kendal Castle's corn mill. The mill served a diversity of industries throughout its life including milling, fulling, snuff, leather and woollen manufacture, suffering more than once from devastating fires, and in 1850 was completely rebuilt, turning to carpet manufacture in 1933.

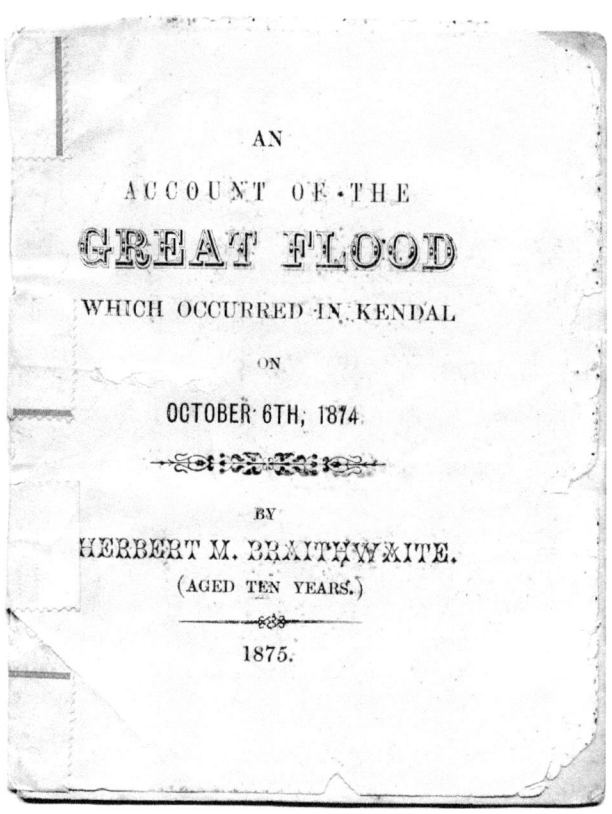

AN

ACCOUNT OF·THE

GREAT FLOOD

WHICH OCCURRED IN KENDAL

ON

OCTOBER 6TH, 1874.

BY

HERBERT M. BRAITHWAITE.

(AGED TEN YEARS.)

1875.

One of the serious river flood years in Kendal, though not the worst, was in 1874. The experience of watching the rising and fast-moving waters so engaged the imagination of young Master Braithwaite that he wrote a graphic and entertaining description which his doting father had printed in the form of a little booklet.

THE GREAT FLOOD

SOME ACCOUNT

OF

THE GREAT FLOOD OF 1874.

It had rained all day, but it was not until night that the water flooded. It began by coming up a drain on the opposite side to Poor House Lane, and it got to nearly four feet on the road. The water then ran two or three yards up Poor House Lane; it ran into a man's house of the name of Eli Cox till it was four feet and a half up the stairs.

Nether Bridge shook with the force of the water; the bridge acted as a barrier, and the water ran over its banks and rushed down the Lound, washing a wall down, to the Toll Bar.

In Stramongate the water rushed right up Mr. Thompson's yard, and into his Schoolroom and Miss Frankland's to the depth of seven inches.

The river floods gave opportunities for boating in streets like Stramongate.

Flooding in the Lound affected workers at the nearby K-Shoes factory. Young women were carried to dry land by young men, to the romantic delight of both parties.

In 1898 the flood waters reached their highest point ever recorded, following a night of torrential rain. Castle Street Girls' School was under 2ft of water and swans were seen swimming serenely in Stramongate where the water at one time reached the height of 8ft and many homes and factories were inundated. Spectators congregated to wonder at the invasive water.

Water has dreadful destructive power and this was demonstrated clearly in the disastrous floods of 1898. Footpaths were torn up, lamp posts and railings were bent and twisted, walls were thrown down and the footbridge across the river at Gooseholme was torn away bodily and completely wrecked.

The nearby Jennings footbridge was also torn down by the floods, providing local children with an exciting sight.

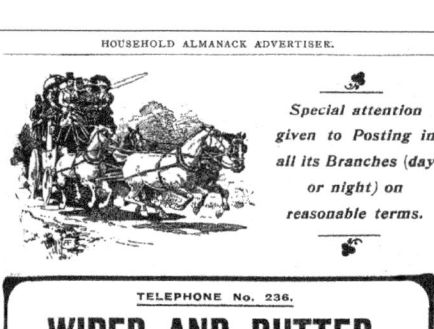

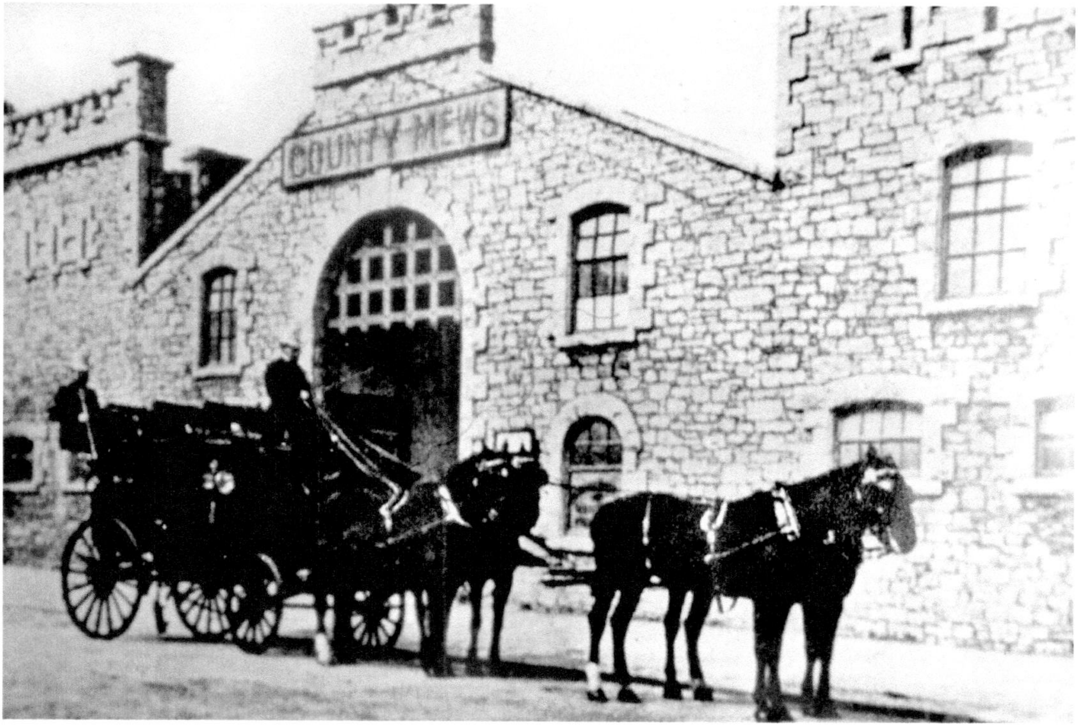
COUNTY MEWS

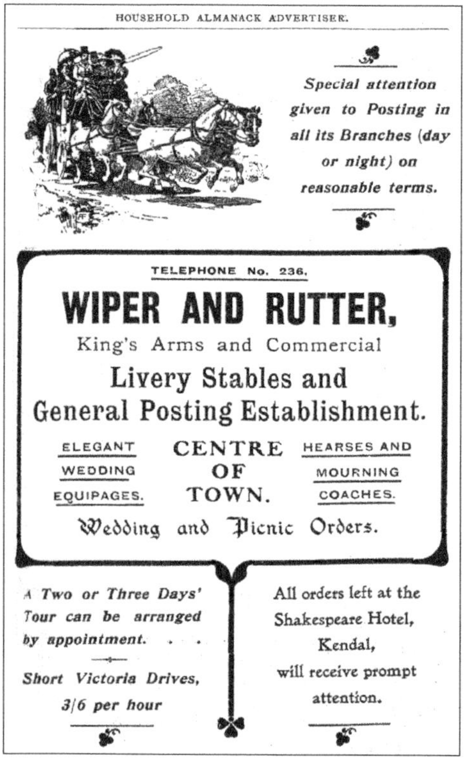
HOUSEHOLD ALMANACK ADVERTISER.
Special attention given to Posting in all its Branches (day or night) on reasonable terms.
TELEPHONE No. 236.
WIPER AND RUTTER,
King's Arms and Commercial
Livery Stables and
General Posting Establishment.
ELEGANT WEDDING EQUIPAGES.
CENTRE OF TOWN.
HEARSES AND MOURNING COACHES.
Wedding and Picnic Orders.
A Two or Three Days' Tour can be arranged by appointment. . .
Short Victoria Drives, 3/6 per hour
All orders left at the Shakespeare Hotel, Kendal, will receive prompt attention.

Above: The County Mews in Sandes Avenue, owned and managed by Albert Simpson, hired out coaches, brakes and gigs of different sizes for funerals, weddings and pleasure parties 'at the most reasonable terms', priding itself on 'strictly observed punctuality'. Horses and conveyances were also hired out for general posting. The mews was taken over by William Wiper in 1917 and in recent years the site has been redeveloped for housing.

Left: The horse carriage reigned supreme in Kendal until the onslaught of the motor car took effect. A number of firms provided transport for various purposes from the humble taxi to and from hotels in the town to great occasions such as weddings. Wiper & Rutter illustrate a stagecoach in their advertisement.

Opposite below: The motorcycle also rose in popularity.

Above: After the end of the First World War the motor car became more popular, the price falling gradually within the reach of more men's pockets. The early models were rugged and less than aesthetically pleasing to modern eyes with the driver and passengers often sitting in the open air as this car in Atkinson & Griffin's garage in Highgate shows.

Tourism has been a major part of the economy of Kendal for a long time. In the days of Wordsworth it was the upper and middle classes who explored the Lakes on foot and horseback. The introduction of the motor coach in the 1920s revolutionised travelling and Kendal became a popular starting point for surveying the wild and primitive fells and enjoying the scenery in relative comfort.

A branch line was opened in 1876 from Hincaster Junction, south of Oxenholme, to connect the main railway line to the coastal line, to enable coke from the north-east to be taken to the ironworks in the Workington and Barrow areas. In 1887 the Royal Train was unexpectedly stopped at the junction when a swarm of bees extinguished a signal lamp.

five

People,
Celebration
and Recreation

Kendal has its share of famous and notable personages. Some, like Thomas de Quincy 'The Opium Eater' and erstwhile editor of *The Westmorland Gazette*, Dr John Dalton the Father of Modern Chemistry and creator of his atomic theory which led to the Periodic Table, and George Romney the artist, are known and celebrated nationally. Others such as John Gough 'The Blind Philosopher', Adam Sedgwick the geologist, and John F. Curwen the architect and historian, are lesser known but highly regarded. Queen Katherine Parr, though not a Kendalian, has been taken to Kendal's heart. During the last few decades Alfred Wainwright, the author of the famous fell-walking guide books, has been integrated into its celebrities.

Kendalians have always loved celebrations. In the seventeenth and eighteenth centuries there were the guild processions when representatives of local trades mounted elaborate displays on carts and, accompanied by bands and hundreds of workmen, paraded through the town. Special occasions like coronations, jubilees, political events, visits by royalty and other prominent persons, were the stimulus for extensive parades. Fairs were eagerly anticipated, especially when held in conjunction with the Hiring Day, where young men often spent their money on fairings – ribbons or trinkets – to give to their sweethearts. Churches and societies held regular events such as lantern lectures and bazaars. There were dinners and balls held in the inns and the Town Hall to celebrate days of historic importance such as the Tercentenary of the Town's Elizabethan Charter and that of William Shakespeare. Yes, Kendal loved to celebrate and did so in great style.

Visits by royalty and other persons of eminence were often celebrated by the building of ceremonial arches over the road at the entrances to the town, the streets and houses being similarly decorated with patriotic motifs, flags and bunting. One such arch was raised at the end of Stramongate Bridge over the road from Scotland. Thomas Carradus fell to his death helping to build a similar arch over Stricklandgate.

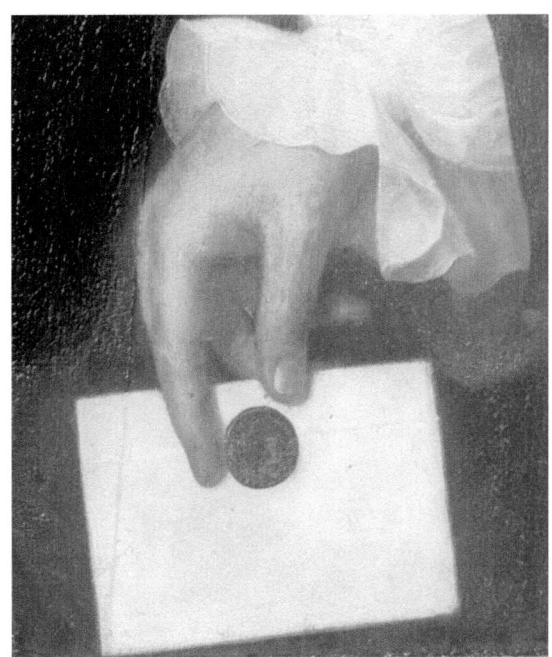

Above left: Although born near Dalton-in-Furness, George Romney is Kendal's most celebrated artist, specialising at first on portraits and family groups. That of the Gower family has pride of place in the Abbot Hall Art Gallery. He married his landlady's daughter, Mary Abbot, and on the marriage certificate he was shown as a face painter.

Above right: His first commission was to paint a little sign for the post office in Kendal depicting a hand holding a letter showing the seal – stamps had not yet been introduced.

Right: He was apprenticed to an artist of lesser merit, Christopher Steele, who had a studio in Redman's Yard where Romney learned the skills of colour mixing and preparation. Dissatisfied with his master, Romney left Steele in 1757 to set up on his own, travelling Europe, mixing with the artistic set and becoming successful. By 1799 he had become senile and returned to Kendal where he died, nursed by his long-suffering wife, in 1802.

Adam Sedgwick was a pioneer biologist. He was born in the village of Dent in 1785 and was naturally clever. He became Professor of Geology at Trinity College, Cambridge, knowing little about the subject, but within eleven years he rose to become president of the Geological Society. He was a charismatic speaker who once kept his audience at the Kendal Literary & Scientific Society spellbound for over two hours.

George Foster Braithwaite, seated on the left of this group of Kendal worthies, was born in 1813 to a family which descended from the Vikings. He set up in business with his brother in 1845 manufacturing woollens in a large mill. He was deeply involved in municipal affairs, becoming Mayor of Kendal no less than six times. Flags were lowered to half-mast throughout the town on his death in 1888.

Typical of the mayors of Kendal, Thomas Baron, a local manufacturer, was mayor in 1888. During his year of office the Lord Mayor of London opened the new grammar school. The Lord Mayor was awarded the Freedom of the Borough and gave a feast of roast beef and plum pudding to the inmates of the workhouse, the hospital and the Howard Home.

One of the oldest treasures preserved in the Mayor's Parlour at the Town Hall is the Cromwellian lantern clock presented by James Cock to the successive mayors of Kendal when he was mayor in 1654. It bears the admonishing inscription, 'Time runneth, your work is before you'.

Left: Thomas Shaw was born in Kendal in 1693 and attended the grammar school. He received an MA degree at Queen's College, Oxford, and was ordained, before being sent as a chaplain to Algiers. After his return to England he became Doctor of Divinity and published books telling of his travels and experiences. He is said to have been of a grotesque appearance but this was countered by his good humour.

Below: He was born in a gabled cottage with a yard known as Lile Capper and died there in 1752. The house was demolished around 1857, in a dilapidated condition, to open up Maude Street. In its later years it housed Agnes Berry's confectionery and cake house. Her husband was well known for giving rides to children in his coal-cart.

Right: Robert Pennington was born in 1858, the son of Job Pennington, and followed him in business as a builder and stonemason. He constructed the stonework of the Job Memorial Mission Hall in Fellside and bought the old prison for £1,000 for use as building material. The demolition was not completed for some twenty years by which time he had died and his son carried on the business.

Below left: The Bazaar Committee published a magazine containing articles on golf and on Ladysmith in the South African War. One issue was produced for each of the three days of the bazaar. Saturday, being Children's Day, it was opened by the young Alice Wakefield.

Below right Bazaars were a popular form of fund-raising for local bodies and causes around the turn of the twentieth century. Robert Pennington was the president of the Kendal Serpentine Golf Club which held an Army & Navy Bazaar in 1901 in aid of club funds. The stalls represented naval battleships and there were exciting scenes of naval battles and army garrisons around the Empire. It raised £358 10s 1d.

John Dawson, seen with his wife Isabella, was an amateur dentist who pulled teeth in the Black Swan public house at the foot of Beast Banks for sixpence a tooth, spending the proceeds on potent liquid refreshment.

He lived in a tall, narrow house at the junction of Low Fellside and Middle Lane. When he returned at night from the Black Swan in a state of intoxication the light from the lamp post in front of his house guided him safely home. It became known as Dawson's Lamp.

Mally Birkett was one of Fellside's great characters. She kept the Rule and Square public house at the bottom of Fountain Brow, a place much frequented by old campaigners of the nineteenth-century wars, until her death in 1882 aged 101! She is said to have gone to war with her husband, been shipwrecked and dragged ashore by a sheep dog.

Charlie Shaw, known as old pee-at (peat) fella, was a well-known character who went daily with his cart to the mosses to bring blocks of peat to sell in the town. Peat was used as fuel instead of coal to heat cottages and houses and to fire bake-house ovens, producing its unmistakeable scent. Charlie was well-known for his distinctive call, 'Ten a penny as lang as we've any.'

KENDAL
Public Wash-house and Baths,
ALL HALLOWS' LANE.

NOTICE IS HEREBY GIVEN,

That the Wash-house and Laundries are open daily (Saturdays and Sundays excepted), from Seven in the Morning to Seven in the Evening.

CHARGES:

1. For any time not exceeding Two Hours, 3d.

2. For each additional Hour, in continuation of the first Two Hours, or part of an Hour, 1½d.

3. Two women occupying the same Stall and the same Drying Horse, will be Charged ONE HALF More.

4. Every Person has a separate Washing Stall, fitted up with two Washing Troughs, a Dolly Tub, when required, and a full supply of Hot and Cold Water, a Pan for boiling their Clothes in, and the use of a Wringing Machine which efficiently throws out the water without the slightest injury to the Clothes, in a twelfth part of the time required by hand. The Clothes after being wrung, are rapidly and thoroughly Dried, in a Closet heated by Steam without the slightest danger of burning. There are powerful and superior Mangles. This Establishment therefore presents advantages, which in point of quickness, economy, and perfection, are unattainable in any private Dwelling.

No Children or other Persons will be admitted, except those actually employed in Washing or otherwise.

THE BATHS

Are open every Working Day from Seven in the Morning till Nine in the Evening, but on Saturdays, during the Summer Months, the time will be extended to Ten in the Evening. The Baths, which are all Private Rooms, consist of Two Classes, each including Hot Cold and Shower Baths, which latter may be made Warm, Tepid, or Cold, as required. The First Class Bath Room, which has a Dressing Room attached, is neatly Carpeted, furnished with two Towels, and all other requisites. The Second Class Bath Rooms, have one Towel, Looking Glass, Bootjack, &c. The utmost attention will be given to maintain thorough cleanliness and good order.

CHARGES FOR ADMISSION:

	First Class.	Second Class.
WARM BATH	1s.	4d.
SHOWER DO.	6d.	3d.
COLD DO.	6d.	3d.

Two Young Persons for one Bath, 2nd Class, Warm 6d., Cold 4d.

THE BATHS FOR FEMALES ARE UP STAIRS AND HAVE A MATRON IN ATTENDANCE.

The time allowed for a First Class Bath is Forty Minutes; for a Second Class Thirty Minutes, beyond that time a double charge will be made.

No Intoxicating Drinks, or Tobacco, allowed on the PREMISES.

All Hallows' Lane, November 5th, 1864.

Wm. Fisher, Printer, Stationer, &c., Kendal.

The local architect, Miles Thompson, designed the public wash-houses and baths which were erected in 1864. They were a boon to local housewives, especially those on Fellside, who could then do their washing more easily. Both men and women could indulge in the luxury of a warm bath, something that was previously denied them in their cramped cottages and houses without running water.

John Watton, the first editor of the K-Shoes
house magazine, was a notable artist, renowned
for his portrait painting. During the Second
World War he was incarcerated in Colditz Castle
from where he sent drawings of prison life
to *The Illustrated London News*. He also forged
German documents and passports for escapees.
He carved faces of his family in relief on the
gatepost of his house in Serpentine Road.

High up on the gable end of 21 Beast Banks
stands the terracotta figure of Miles Thompson,
the Kendal architect, holding an architect's
plan and looking across to where stood the
National School for Boys. Miles started work
as a draughtsman for the Webster architects
and took over the business after about twenty
years. He designed many important buildings
in Kendal. One, the Wash-House, has become a
public house, named after him.

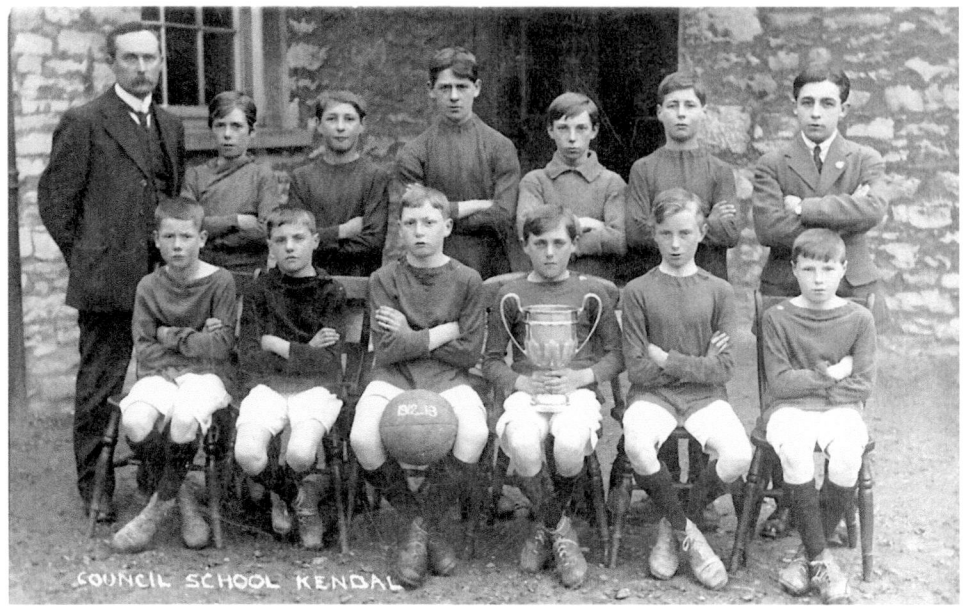

Sport was taken seriously by schools in the twentieth century and every boys' school had its football team which entered the local championships. Great was the jubilation when they won. Castle Street Boys' School won the cup in 1913 and proudly hold it for the photograph.

Kendal High School was keen on playing netball. The under-15s team were champions in 1946. From left to right, back row: Delia Towers, Margaret Webster, -?-. Front row: Pamela Bacon, Irene Wilson, Lena Simpson, Jennifer Temple.

Thomas Sandes founded a school in Sandes Hospital for poor boys of the town who were prepared for apprenticeship or to enter the grammar school. At one time the boys learned weaving and carding and sold their products. By 1714 the blue uniform was introduced and girls were admitted. By 1838 their number equalled that of the boys. The boys' school merged with the new grammar school in 1886.

Kendal Grammar School organised an annual cross-country race to the Helme and back in which all the boys took part. They are seen at the start, running past the old toll house outside the school. The end of the race saw the customary tail of tired strugglers but most of the boys enjoyed the event.

The 300th anniversary of the granting of the Elizabethan Charter was celebrated in great style. The town was brilliantly illuminated and decorated and triumphal arches were erected across the roads through which passed a grand procession of representatives of the town's industries together with the Friendly Societies and Sunday school children. There were fireworks on Gooseholme and three memorial trees were planted on High Beast Banks.

Left: Medals were given to the children to mark the Queen's Jubilee in 1897 and the town's Tercentenary in 1875, which they wore with pride when taking part in the grand parades. Similar medals were given to mark other special occasions and were awarded to school children who had registered no absence or lateness during a whole year.

Opposite below: Fancy dress parades and competitions were a prominent feature in many celebrations for which the winners were amply rewarded with a prize. Whether taking part in events or just watching, visiting sweets stalls or patronising the refreshment tents, occasions like the K-Shoes Fête were red-letter days for all.

Above: In the 1930s K-Shoes held an annual fête with a 'K-Queen'. With her attendants she led a procession of decorated floats, mostly horse-drawn, through the town to the cricket field where she was crowned. It was an occasion looked forward to with great anticipation and raised funds for the hospital.

Tom O'Loughlin was Mayor of Kendal in 1952. As was traditional, the celebrations on Mayor-making Day included a procession. The Sea Scouts paraded and marched past the Town Hall in his honour.

Colonel Weston MP unveiled the War Memorial at the head of Market Place in July 1920. The bronze statue of an infantryman by the sculptor C.W. Coombs stands atop a stone plinth looking into the town. Many sad memories were evoked of the 316 men slaughtered in the conflict whose names are recorded on the memorial. Over 1,000 people, with a choir of children, watched the proceedings.

The first May Day Parade in Kendal was held in 1883. It was bright with sunshine and many hundreds came in from the country to watch the procession of horses and carriages, all cleaned and polished with the horses' tails and manes plaited with bright-coloured ribbons and the trade carts showing off merchandise. It was a great success but did not last for many years.

Horses were trotted up and down New Road at the Horse Fair, weaving in and out of the crowds with the occasional accident. Transactions were sealed with a thwack of the hands or by the giving of a luck penny. Once sold, there was no returning the horse if it was unsatisfactory. It was up to the purchaser not to buy a 'pig in a poke'.

Chipperfield's Circus passes through Longpool. When the circus came to town many children took an unofficial half-holiday to watch the parade. Strange animals like elephants and camels, cages on carts containing lions and other fierce animals, clowns and horses with riders in their costumes, all excited the imagination when they processed from the railway station to the circus ground.

Fairs have been a feature of Kendal life from the earliest days. By the nineteenth century they had been regularised into a spring and an autumn fair with specialised fairs for cattle, horses, fruit and vegetables at seasonal times. The open space alongside the river on New Road was the venue for the amusement fairs where the traditional roundabouts, swings, stalls and booths were gathered. Kendal still enjoys fun there.

Easter was the time for traditional pastimes of which rolling Pache eggs down Castle Hill was one. Eggs were a sign of new life or the Resurrection of Jesus Christ The eggs were hard boiled and dyed or painted in pretty patterns. The children assembled at the top of the hill and released their eggs. The one which rolled furthest without cracking was the winner.

Winters can be hard in Kendal and that in 1895 was especially so. The first sign of snow brought out sledges on the hills and heavy frost froze the river for days on end; ice on the canal was four inches thick for weeks. Canal water was used to flood the area known now as Rinkfield to provide an excellent skating rink for the Kendal Skating Club.

Above: Cycling became very popular among both women and men in the later nineteenth century. The Kendal Amateur Bicycle Club was formed which held an annual dinner, sports and races. Cycling rallies drew crowds of hundreds of participants and there were cycle gymkhanas and parades. A cycle and fancy dress parade, with prizes, was held in 1901 in aid of the Consumptive Sanatorium, raising £63 15s 10d.

Left: The motorcycle gave greater freedom for longer journeys than the humble bicycle. Clubs were formed and rallies and trials were held. Some, more adventurous, even travelled as far as the Forth Bridge in Scotland.

Lady Bagot's Own (1st Kendal) was the first Boy Scout group in the town and an early one in the country. The boys are seen here proudly on parade with Lady Bagot in the gardens of Levens Hall.

The Kendal Rifle Volunteers were local forces who were trained in soldiering. They took part in displays and processions and held annual camps, often in Kendal Castle. Many joined with the regular army during the Boer War. In 1885 they were equipped with Martini Henry rifles and competed in local and national shooting competitions. They won the Belgian Cup on Wimbledon Common in 1886.

Rugby football matches were first played in Kendal in 1872. The premier club was The Kendal Hornets which was highly successful in the game and attracted large crowds to watch it play. Most of the players at that time were factory or mill workers. The Kendal Rugby Club played in Maude's Meadow until 1929 when the lease ended. The meadow is now the quiet Noble's Rest pleasure park.

There were two golf courses in Kendal, one on the old race course on Scout Scar and the other on Cunswick Scar which moved to The Heights near Serpentine Walks. The two clubs combined in 1907 as the Kendal Golf Club and a proposition in that year to play on Sundays was unanimously turned down. The club went on to prosper into the present day.

Dr T. Howard Somervell achieved fame in 1924 when he accompanied Mallory on the ill-fated attempt to climb to the summit of Mount Everest He took supplies of Kendal Mint Cake with him. On his return he gave a number of illustrated lectures about the mountain and the expedition and on 12 February 1948 he was granted the Freedom of the Borough.

Smoking tobacco was considered a natural habit for men and for some women throughout the nineteenth and twentieth centuries until recent years and men often came together in clubs or groups to enjoy it. Smoking concerts, often with a supper, were held to raise funds or to get together to enjoy smoking. When he resigned, the manager of the gas works, Mr Ritson, was given a smoker's cabinet.

The Howard Orphan Home was established by the Hon. Mary Howard of Levens in 1865 for orphan girls of Westmorland. It was for those girls preferably from the Kendal Workhouse, and as a house for girls and women who had left the workhouse for domestic service, and were out of work through sickness. The home accommodated forty girls and was designed so that it did not have the appearance of a workhouse.

The Allen Technical Institute, adjacent to Kendal Museum, was formally opened in 1914 with a ceremony shortened on account of the start of the First World War. The name is a tribute to James Allen of Kirkby Lonsdale, one of Kendal's greatest philanthropists, who was in business in the town for over sixty years. He died in 1896 and his trust gave some £10,000 towards the building of the Institute.

Right: The Serpentine Walks was a pleasure ground set up in 1824, with leafy glades and flowerbeds where people could stroll around and enjoy picnics on payment of an admission charge. Twenty-five years later they were thrown over free to the public, Kendal's first municipal park. The haunt of squirrels, owls and other birds with a large variety of wild flowers and magnificent trees, the Walks became very popular.

Below: One of the attractions in the Serpentine Walks on the high Kendal Fell above the town was the summer house. Children called it the cuckoo house on account of the typical sound made when they shouted through the keyhole. There was a well nearby reputed to have curative properties. The caretaker bottled and sold the water which people actively believed promoted their well-being.

On the high point of Scout Scar overlooking the Lyth Valley, a shelter was constructed in 1912 to commemorate the coronation of King George V. With its domed roof it soon received the nickname of The Mushroom. High up, under the roof, is a panorama in silhouette of the surrounding area on which all the major points of interest are shown.

At a number of places around the town can still be seen archways in south-facing walls. They are bee boles, places where straw bee skeps, a form of beehive, were placed to shelter from the weather. Bees were kept by many people to provide a supply of honey for sweetening food in the days when sugar was scarce and expensive.

On 2 June 1953, happy crowds filled Abbot Hall Park to celebrate the coronation of Queen Elizabeth II. Sea Cadets in uniform take pride of place.

The 1930s brought more leisure time for ordinary working people and they began to enjoy excursions into the country or the seaside, often organised by works or social organisations. In a roofless charabanc, with the wind in their hair, they could be whisked away for a happy day together and be refreshed to face again the daily grind.

Other local titles published by The History Pess

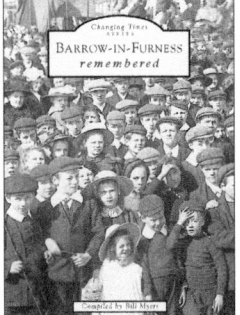

Barrow-in-Furness Remembered
BILL MYERS

Barrow-in-Furness has experienced an astonishing transformation from a village to a major industrial town over the past 150 years. This book reveals the stories behind this growth through contemporary newspaper headlines and reports. Digging for iron, steelmaking, shipbuilding, the growth of the railways and the laying of tram lines are described in articles and historical notes drawn from a number of newspapers once published in the town.

978 0 7524 2083 7

Whitehaven Then & Now Volume II
ALAN ROUTLEDGE

This collection of over 85 pairs of images reveals some of the changes that have taken place in Whitehaven during the last century. Streets and buildings, organisations, shops and churches are shown as they used to be. Each pair is accompanied by informative text containing historical detail and local information sure to appeal to both the long-established resident and the interested visitor.

978 0 7524 3094 2

Lancaster and District
SUSAN ASHWORTH AND NIGEL DALZIEL

This portrait of a period at once familiar and remote includes views of the historic city of Lancaster, illustrates the development of Morecambe from a small fishing community to a thriving seaside resort, recaptures the wealth of Morecambe Bay's maritime history, and explores the attractive villages of the Lune Valley. For those who can still remember, it offers a trip down memory lane; for others, it is a voyage of discovery.

978 0 7524 4964 7

Millom Remembered
BILL MYERS

This fascinating and detailed book delves into 150 years of growth and change in the town of Millom on the West Cumberland coast. Millom is fortunate in having many newspapers which have left a comprehensive record of its daily life. Bill Myers is assistant editor for the *North West Evening Mail* and writes the 'Memories' page. The 100 illustrations show the development of the North West over the past century and are drawn from his private collection of postcards and photographs.

978 0 7524 3386 8

If you are interested in purchasing other books published by The History Press, or in case you have difficulty finding any of our books in your local bookshop, you can also place orders directly through our website

www.thehistorypress.co.uk